"I've had the pleasure of knowing Melitsa Waage for over a decade, and from the moment I met her, I knew she was an ambitious, hardworking, and intelligent young woman. She has worked her way up from the VIP service industry in Las Vegas, to become a success in a number of different industries. You're a badass Melitsa, and I know you will continue to accomplish great things in this world."

-Dana White, UFC President

Detoxify Your Mind

GAIN CLARITY AND CONTROL OF YOUR THOUGHTS TO UNLOCK YOUR FULL POTENTIAL

MELITSA WAAGE

ISBN: 978-1-951503-10-9 (Ebook)
ISBN: 978-1-951503-11-6 (Paperback)

 AUTHORSUNITE

Published by Authorsunite.com

Tables of contents

About the Author:

Who is Melitsa Waage?

Transformational Thought Leader
International Speaker
Fitness Champion
Adventurer
Thrill Seeker
World Traveler
Author
Motivational Speaker

Her obsession with helping others began when she was just a little girl: a child with a "dark" life and no real hopes of any successes in her future, with heroin addict parents, forced into the foster care system, mentally abused and constantly being reminded she was not good enough, and that she would never amount to anything or achieve anything.

Despite these adversities she knew she was destined for more. She knew she was created for greatness! She used her troubled past as a beacon of hope, sharing her story with the world and letting people know, "Things don't happen to you, they happen for you."

Her message is clear: she wants you to know that, no matter what has happened in your life, you can rise up, conquer your life, and create the life of your dreams if you allow that to happen.

Her dedication to helping others has led to multiple business endeavors, which are her ways of "paying it forward" to those in need and individuals who are looking to amplify their lives and create the life of their dreams.

Backpack Attack is Melitsa's initiative that gifts backpacks filled with daily supplies to children in orphanages, designed to improve the quality of life of children in need.

Epic Life Mastermind is a platform for young entrepreneurs to network on a monthly basis, to share their ideas, to take their businesses to the next level, and to hold each other accountable for their progress.

The Detoxify Your Mind App is an interactive program assisting individuals with the elimination of "toxic" thoughts and behaviors holding them back from creating a fulfilling, extraordinary lives, and living to one's full potential. (Coming Soon) Nov 2018

The latter two ventures are Melitsa's exclusive platforms for the individuals with the desire to experience their lives and minds at their peak performance.

Her method of self-development caters to those who understand that fulfillment in life and mindset go hand-in-hand. The main idea behind all of Melitsa's creations is living an extraordinary life is a choice we all make ourselves.

Are you willing to commit to the life of your dreams? Melitsa Waage believes she can assist you on this exciting path.

Preface

I was inspired to write this book after receiving countless messages from people needing help taking their life to the next level. People feeling stuck with no clarity, no vision and no desire to succeed in life.

Most of them have zero lack of motivation, aren't feeling inspired and are having a mental struggle every day when it comes to their life and things that matter to them. In this action guide book, I reveal my secrets and daily habits that I have used to amplify my life.

I have always had an obsession with helping others. My obsession with helping others began when I was just a little girl.

A child with a dark life and no real hopes of any successes in my future. Coming from HEROIN addict parents, forced into the foster care system, mentally abused and constantly being reminded I wasn't good enough and that I would never amount to anything. Regardless of these adversities, I knew I was destined for more, I knew I was going to create GREATNESS in my life.

I've used my troubled past to become a beacon of hope, wanting to share my story with the world and let people know..."Things don't happen to you, They happen for You"

My message to the world is that no matter what has happened in your life you can rise up, conquer your life and create the life of your dreams if you allow it!!!

I want to help you reach your full potential, maximize your talents and help you step into your power and walk into your GREATNESS!!!

Thank you for allowing me into your life!

Let's MAKE THIS HAPPEN!!!

With lots of love in my heart,

- Melitsa Waage

Introduction

In this action guide book (Detoxify Your Mind), I want to simplify the process of creating an extraordinary life, a life of fulfillment, joy, purpose, a life you never thought possible.

I know it is attainable because I have used all of these secret ingredients to create the life of my dreams. I have done it and I am living proof that this information works.

Regardless of your current situation, how you feel in life right now, or what your daily habits are, I believe you can implement what's in this book and use it to create an extraordinary life.

I have made a commitment to my life and it is to serve and help people step into their greatness! In the next five years, I'm on a mission to serve one million people through my programs, books, workshops and masterminds.

Welcome to our journey!

Chapter 1

Defining You

"WHAT ARE YOU WILLING TO DO TO CREATE
THE LIFE OF YOUR DREAMS?"

MELITSA WAAGE

In this chapter, we will go through five phases:

Phase 1:
Defining who you really are at this moment in your life.

Phase 2:
Defining who you want to become.

Phase 3:
Defining what in life sets your heart on fire? What inspires you?

Phase 4:
You will write a description of your life in five years from now.

Phase 5:
Awareness Assessment

1

Phase 1
Defining You

No Matter what you have gone through, you can create an amazing life!

I.   This life is yours!! Happiness, love, fulfillment, purpose is all up for the taking. It's your choice!

II. How bad do you want it? That's what it all boils down to. You're one decision away from making it a reality.

III. I want to inspire you and help you visualize the life of your dreams, and make you realize that your visualization can come true!!!

Answer these questions truthfully in two sentences. Be honest with yourself.

Who are you at this moment in your life?

_____

_____

_____

_____

_____

Are you happy with your life? If yes, please explain. If no, Please explain.

_____

_____

_____

_____

_____

What bad habits do you have?

_____

_____

_____

_____

_____

What good habits do you have?

_____

_____

_____

_____

_____

What kind of environments do you spend time in?

_____

_____

_____

_____

_____

Who are the top three people you hang out with?

_____

_____

_____

_____

_____

What kind of lifestyle are you living in?

_____

_____

_____

_____

_____

Can you succeed in the kind of lifestyle you're living in? If yes, please explain. If no, please explain.

_____

_____

_____

_____

_____

Are you 100% happy with your life?
If "YES" please explain, if "NO" please explain.

_____

_____

_____

_____

_____

What changes do you need to make in your life so you can start feeling happiness, fulfillment, and progress? (Be specific.)

_____

_____

_____

_____

We become a product of our environment, that's why it's important we protect our energy and our space. Surround yourself with amazing people, people who inspire you and bring out the best in you. Don't settle for mediocrity!

Phase 2
Defining who you want to be!

"LOVING WHAT YOU DO IS MUCH MORE
IMPORTANT THaN WHAT YOU ACTUALLY DO!"

Who are the TOP THREE people that inspire you?

- a)
- b)
- c)

Why do they inspire you? (Be specific.) Is it the way they look, the way they speak, the way they carry themselves?

_____

_____

_____

_____

_____

_____

_____

_____

_____

_____

_____

I'VE NOT CEASED BEING FEARFUL. I'VE GONE
AHEAD DESPITE THE POUNDING IN MY HEART
THAT SAYS;

TURN BACK, TURN BACK, YOU'LL DIE IF YOU GO
TOO FAR.

ERICA JONG

Write down 3 new daily habits you will implement to progress in your life.

- a)
- b)
- c)

Write down 3 negative bad habits you need to get rid of so you can see progress in your life.

- a)
- b)
- c)

Write down 3 things you want to accomplish in the next 30 days.

- a)
- b)
- c)

Be specific about your plans and what must you do to get these three things completed in the next thirty days.

Explain exactly how you are going to carry it out step by step.

- Step 1:

  _____

  _____

  _____

- Step 2:

  _____

  _____

  _____

- Step 3:

  _____

  _____

  _____

- Step 4:

  _____

  _____

  _____

- Step 5:

  _____

  _____

  _____

- Step 6:

  _____

  _____

  _____

- Step 7:

  _____

  _____

  _____

- Step 8:

  _____

  _____

  _____

- Step 9:

  _____

  _____

  _____

- Step 10:

  _____

  _____

  _____

Phase 3
Defining what sets your heart on fire and what you're passionate about!

IF I GET STUCK IN WHO I AM NOW, I WILL
NEVER BLOSSOM INTO WHO I MIGHT YET
BECOME. I NEED TO PRACTICE THE ART OF
LETTING GO.

- SAM KEEN

What would you do for a living if you knew success was guaranteed?

_____

_____

_____

_____

What would you do for a living if you had all the money in the world?

_____

_____

_____

_____

What would you love to do even if it never led to success?

_____

_____

_____

_____

If these three answers match... Then most certainly this is the thing you should be pursuing wholeheartedly.

What helped me figure out my passion and purpose was answering these three questions.

What would I do for living if I knew success was guaranteed?

<u>My answer:</u>
I love helping people and being of service. When I help someone in need or when I do a good gesture it makes my heart feel good. It's a feeling of deep satisfaction that I get when I help someone or when I'm being of service to a person.

What would I do for a living if I had all the money in the world?

<u>My answer:</u>
My answer is the same. I would be in service to the world and continue to build companies that help individuals reach their peak potential by shifting their mindsets to overcome any self-limiting beliefs.

What would I do for living even if I knew it didn't lead to success?

<u>My answer:</u>
I'm doing it right now! Helping people! I'm creating courses, programs, masterminds that are helping people find clarity, purpose and passion in their lives.

These answers should match!

Doesn't matter what kind of life you are living or how much money you have in the bank. Your living situation shouldn't change your mind on what your passion in life is.

If your answers matched, then all that's left is for you to turn that desire into an obsession! You are the only one that can make this happen! Don't waste anymore time. Start today, start researching on how you can make that desire a reality. Be relentless until you see your desire come to fruition. Everything starts with baby steps. Little by little. The key is to stay committed, determined, and never give up!

I can't wait to see what you create!!!

Phase 4
Write a description of your life in five years from now.

YOUR WORK IS TO DISCOVER YOUR WORK,
AND THEN, WITH ALL YOUR HEART, TO GIVE
YOURSELF TO IT.

-BUDDHA

Write a description of the life you hope to create in five years from now.
(Be specific and dare to dream big)

_____

_____

_____

_____

_____

_____

_____

_____

_____

_____

_____

_____

Manifest, declare, and visualize what you want for your life and work your ass off to attain those things. It's not meant to be easy. It's meant to be worth it! What we do is a critical part of who we are and who we want to become. What you procrastinate or not act upon, defines you too; determining the person you will never become.

I don't understand how it's ok for people to not want to live their best self or create the life of their dreams when we only have one life to live. How could you not want to become the best version of yourself or even worse, how could you not want to work for the things you really want in life. I would hate to get old and be on my death bed wishing I would've had the courage to make my dreams come true.

I would hate for anyone to have to go through that agony. I believe the graveyard is the richest place on earth. So many shattered and broken dreams people took to the grave because they were too afraid to fail or they didn't want to put in the work to see their dreams come to life!

Don't let this be you!!!

Phase 5
Awareness Assessment

THIS IS THE SINGLE MOST POWERFUL
INVESTMENT WE CAN EVER MAKE IN LIFE,
INVESTMENT IN OURSELVES, IN THE ONLY
INSTRUMENT WE HAVE WHICH TO DEAL WITH
LIFE AND TO CONTRIBUTE.

-STEPHEN R. COVEY

List three principles that affect your life daily. In what ways are you affected? Do they impact you in positive or negative ways?

1.

_____

_____

_____

_____

_____

2.

_____

_____

_____

_____

_____

3.

_____

_____

_____

_____

_____

Always be aware on how things are affecting your life!

Awareness Assessment:

This assessment will show you where you are in life and what areas you should focus on for your progress. To help with your progress, retake this assessment when you're done with this book. On these pages, read each statement and circle the number that best indicates the statement. This will help keep you aware of the important things and also help you create better decisions for your daily progress. Circle the number on how well you perform.

(1 being very poor and 10 being outstanding)

1. My focus goes towards the things I can do something about rather than the things I have no control over.

   1   2   3   4   5   6   7   8   9   10

2. I stay true to my word and honor my promises and commitments.

   1   2   3   4   5   6   7   8   9   10

3. I have my life under control.

    1   2   3   4   5   6   7   8   9   10

4. I maintain a well balanced life - Family, friends, work and so forth.

    1   2   3   4   5   6   7   8   9   10

5. When working on a task, I am considerate of other people's concerns and needs.

    1   2   3   4   5   6   7   8   9   10

6. I work extremely hard at everything I do, but I do not burn myself out.

    1   2   3   4   5   6   7   8   9   10

7. I do not speak negatively about others when they are not present.

    1   2   3   4   5   6   7   8   9   10

8. I show compassion and consideration towards others.

    1   2   3   4   5   6   7   8   9   10

9. I'm sensitive to the feelings of others.

    1   2   3   4   5   6   7   8   9   10

10. My daily routines are meaningful and contribute to my overall goals in life.

    1   2   3   4   5   6   7   8   9   10

11. I take full responsibility for my emotions rather than blame others or my circumstances.

    1   2   3   4   5   6   7   8   9   10

12. I work well with others.

    1   2   3   4   5   6   7   8   9   10

13. I am 100% certain on what I want to accomplish in my life.

    1   2   3   4   5   6   7   8   9   10

14. I seek advice from mentors and people whom I value and respect.

    1   2   3   4   5   6   7   8   9   10

15. I care about my physical health and work on it every day.

    1   2   3   4   5   6   7   8   9   10

16. I take time to nurture my life.

    1   2   3   4   5   6   7   8   9   10

17. I take the time to build and improve my relationships with others.

    1   2   3   4   5   6   7   8   9   10

18. I am open to listening to other people's opinions.

    1   2   3   4   5   6   7   8   9   10

19. I care about other people's success including my own.

    1   2   3   4   5   6   7   8   9   10

20. I am disciplined in carrying out plans (avoiding procrastination, productivity killers, and so forth.)

    1   2   3   4   5   6   7   8   9   10

Before you continue, add all the numbers you circled.
Write your total number in this space _____
Score Board:
160+: You have some work to do. I want you to focus on becoming more aware of your actions.

Think to yourself if what you're about to do or say will have a positive effect on your life. Focus on being a person of contribution. Make it a habit to stay committed to the things you say you will do. People dislike individuals they can't count on. It makes no one look good.

120 to 160: You have improvements to make but you're not bad. Take baby steps in improving the quality of your life, it all doesn't have to happen in one day. Progress brings happiness, stay committed and focused on your goals. You have nothing to lose and everything to gain.

120 or less: You are doing great! However, in order to continue feeling and doing great, you must continue to explore and be on a constant pursuit of growth and evolution. Never get comfortable. If you snooze you will lose!

If you have a high score, don't beat yourself up! Now you are aware and you know the changes you need to make in order to change your negative habits.

Progress brings happiness, so start implementing the changes little by little and get ready to watch your life transform in ways you never thought possible.

Chapter 2

There Is Beauty In The Storm

This is the single most powerful investment we can ever make in life, investment in ourselves, in the only instrument we have which to deal with life and to contribute.

-Stephen r. Covey

Are you finding yourself in a hard place in your life right now?

Are you struggling with depression, loneliness, anxiety, fear, confidence, worthiness or constantly in a battle with your mind?

These feelings are the body trying to communicate with you there is something wrong. These are clues your body is talking to you and letting you know that you must be nourished. Your mind, your spirit, and your soul need love and attention.

I can assure you that you are not alone. It may seem the world is falling at your feet, you feel depleted, defeated and nowhere to run and hide. You feel consumed by negativity and trying to escape your daily struggle. I UNDERSTAND! I have been there.

I will share a personal story with you. Not many people know. For many years I was embarrassed, ashamed and afraid of what people would think or say until I realized that my truth would set me free!

Four years ago, I walked away from a man that I was with for nine years. This man was my husband, my best friend, and my everything for almost a decade. I thought this man was the love of my life, oh boy, was I wrong. People used to ask us to write a book about our marriage since they perceived us to be the perfect couple. I also thought it was amazing at the time as well because I didn't know any better.

For a decade I supported this man and I was the breadwinner in the relationship. I paid the bills, we drove expensive cars and lived in beautiful homes. All of that luxury out of my own pockets. We started multiple businesses together and I was the investor in each one. Long story short, our businesses were not providing the type of return we needed in order to continue to operate them.

He then was forced to go out and find a real job and make some money to provide for our lavish lifestyle. At the time, it was the breath of fresh air I needed because I could use some help paying for all of our investments, bills, and everyday living but that breathe was short lived.

I helped him land a job making really good money. Within 3 months of him in his new job, he started cheating on me. Not with just one girl but with at least 5 I know of. People ask me, "how did you know?"

For some reason, I felt it in my heart. The man I was once in love with was no longer there. It was as if he vanished. Nowhere to find him, to me he was dead.

When I looked into his eyes, it seemed I was looking into the eyes of a dead man. I remember one night I knew for a fact he lied about where he was and who he was with. I had living proof he was lying in front of me. When I got home with the thought he was cheating on me... I was consumed with pain. A pain I can't even explain nor comprehend.

My emotions, my fear, and my wrath took over me and I jumped on him and began to hit him... I was screaming at the top of my lungs saying "how could you do this to me"? "You're cheating on me"..."How could you"? It was like I was in a living nightmare. A horrible dream I wanted to wake up from but I couldn't. I was stuck in the pit of hell with an agonizing pain with nowhere to go and nowhere to run.

He was holding me back and assuring me that I was crazy and I was making everything up in my head.

It got to where he actually convinced me that I had made everything up. That nothing was true and it was a complete misunderstanding.

The craziest thing is that I actually apologized for jumping on him and hitting him. Then the nightmare begins.

This was his opportunity to use what I did to him against me and the relationship. He said he didn't know if this relationship could work because I hit him, he said he would leave town for a few days because he needed to be away from me to think if he still wanted this marriage.

You can only imagine the state of mind I was in. I was blaming myself every single day. My mind was poisoned... How could I do this to him? I ruined my marriage. I ruined my life... these were the things I was telling myself every day. I lost fifteen pounds in two weeks. I looked lifeless. I looked sick and like a skeleton. It was awful. For two months I suffered. He was distant and emotionally unavailable. But one day it all changed like a switch. He said, "Babe, I love you and we are going to work things out." That was like music to my ears. My world was happy again, so I thought.

The happiness was short lived. One night he got home intoxicated. And for the first time in nine years, I had the eager sensation to check his phone while he was passed out. The first text message read "I miss you, I wish I was laying next to you caressing and kissing you."

My life froze once again. I felt my heart beat stop for a moment. My world shattered once again. I woke him up by smacking his legs and screaming "who is this" "who is this" "who is this"?????

I started running down the stairs of our four story condo in desperation and crying barely being able to breathe. He screamed, "Melitsa give me my phone" ... that's all he cared about was to have his phone. I hid the phone somewhere in the kitchen but I pretended to have it behind me with my hands holding it.

We were going back and forth and I was begging him to tell me who was the girl he had sent that text to. He kept telling me she was nobody and he was just flirting and she meant nothing: she was nobody to him. This discussion went on for hours while I was on the floor crying and bawling my eyes out.

Finally, I found the courage to get up from the floor. He kept asking me for his phone and I told him I had thrown it in the upstairs closet as I was running down the stairs. So he went looking for it. The moment he went up the stairs, I grabbed my car keys and ran as fast as I could to my car with his phone in my hand. The craziest thing is that I had my car in a private garage and I had to wait for that garage door to open. It was taking forever!!

As I'm waiting, I see him running towards me and the car... the garage was slowly opening, he managed to almost get to the car but I sped away before he could. I drove about 1 mile away from our home and then I stopped and looked at his phone.

I found the craziest texts from over five women. Talking about how he would like to fuck them and get hotel rooms for them. Naked pictures of their private parts and his private parts too. This man was a monster. It was almost as if I had been married to a complete stranger.

What happened next?

I called all the girls on the text messages and pictures. Most answered immediately. I told them what was happening.

They were in shock and couldn't believe it. They were telling me he was saying he was trying to get a divorce and that his wife was trying to take away everything. He was fooling them all. Once I hung up the phone with them, I calmed myself down. I said to myself that yes this is happening and how am I going to deal with it. Am I going to allow this to destroy me or am I going to rule this situation?

I remember at that moment I was accepting it. So I drove back to my home. I felt a sense of peace inside me. Something inside me saying "Melitsa, you are an incredible woman and you do not deserve this."

I looked at him and I said: "Chris, you will never see me lay in your bed again."

I packed only my clothes and my dogs and I left my condo that day. I never ever looked back. I was sleeping on a friend's couch for three months while I figured out what I was going to do. This was the DARKEST moment of my life. Everything I knew for almost a decade vanished. My life, my home, my "best friend", "soulmate", books, furniture, years of work, my businesses... EVERYTHING GONE!

Where do I go from here I asked myself?

Little did I know that God had something so much greater and more incredible for me. A life that I could have never dreamed of. Opportunities and people that would make me look at this world as a better place. I came to understand that this man I once called my husband was really my anchor to mediocrity.

After leaving him, my life has amplified and gotten better tenfold. I love everything about my life! I'm passionate about my work, I'm passionate about the people I surround myself with, I'm passionate about impacting people's lives and helping them realize how amazing and incredible they are, regardless of the adversities they have had to endure.

If it weren't for this betrayal, you wouldn't be here reading this book. So many amazing things have come out of that horrible situation. I've had the opportunity to really dive into personal development and really dig into the core of who I am.

I've had the opportunity to create movements like "Backpack Attack" that gifts backpacks filled with daily supplies to children in orphanages, designed to improve the quality of life of children in need. I also recently started the Epic Talks Miami, a platform for young entrepreneurs to network on a monthly basis, share their ideas, and take their businesses to the next level while holding each other accountable for their progress.Women's Success Academy is another project I'm passionate about and I can go on and on about the exciting things that are happening. As I said before, my mission is to serve 5 million lives in the next five years through my programs, books, workshops, and masterminds.

My passion is helping people and my purpose is to create programs that could be a vehicle to help people all over the world find their purpose and passion so they can step into their greatness. I believe with my story I can move mountains! I want my legacy to be "Because of her work I never gave up."So this is why I want you to believe, and trust in your process and in your journey. Find the lesson in your storm. In this book, I'm going to show you exactly all the tools and secret ingredients I used to create the life I live now and it just keeps getting better!

YOU ARE NOT ALONE!!!!!

THERE IS BEAUTY IN THE STORM!

Chapter 3

Success Rituals

THE ONLY QUESTION THAT MATTERS

"AM I LIVING IN A WAY THAT IS DEEPLY
SATISFYING AND TRULY EXPRESSES ME?"

- CARL ROGERS

OUR DEEPEST FEAR IS NOT THAT WE ARE
INADEQUATE. OUR DEEPEST FEAR IS THAT WE
ARE POWERFUL BEYOND MEASURE. IT IS OUR
LIGHT, NOT OUR DARKNESS, THAT FRIGHTENS
US.

-NELSON MANDELA

Morning Ritual #1

In Morning Rituals, I will help you create new morning habits to set your day up for success. Keep committed to these rituals and to your growth!

From the moment you wake up, before you look at your phone and before you get out of bed, I want you to grab your journal and write down five things you are grateful for. Then explain why you are grateful for them, you can also say things you are grateful for that you still have not accomplished in your life. Use these daily gratitudes as a manifestation exercise.

For example, today I am grateful for my platform DETOXIFY YOUR LIFE being the number one personal-development platform in the world. I want to continue inspiring individuals to find their purpose and passion in life so they can step into their greatness!! - Melitsa Waage

That is an example of how you can write down your daily gratitudes and manifestations.

Morning Ritual #2

Ten Minutes of Meditation!

I know what you might be thinking "I hate meditation" or "I can't meditate". Trust me, I used to say the same thing. I practice ten minutes of meditation every morning to set my intention for the day. I tell myself what kind of day I would like to create for myself, what goals do I want to accomplish, how many people can I be of service to today?

This will help you gain a lot of clarity in your life and it will also help you tremendously to have a positive and more fulfilling day.

I use an app called HeadSpace. Download it on your phone and get started with your meditation ritual. I promise you will love it!

Morning Ritual #3

MAKE YOUR BED!!

The moment your feet hit the ground, turn your body around and make your bed.

Following these 3 new rituals will set you up for daily success. Within the first 30 mins of waking up, you have already accomplished 3 important things.

Starting your day off on such a positive note will allow you to continue a positive kind of day. Slaying through the day, becoming more effective, more assertive, happier, with more clarity. In this state of mind we become more confident, more aware and more in tune with ourselves.

Morning Ritual #4

When getting ready and dressed for work, work on setting your mind up for success by playing a morning motivational video or listen to something that inspires you and gets you excited. What works for me is YOUTUBE! I love this vessel of communication. In the search button I search for "Morning Motivation" and there are thousands of videos you can listen to as you prepare yourself. I stay away from listening to the news or any negativity. Feed your mind what you want and stay away from information or energy you don't want.

Manifest, declare, and visualize what you want for your life and work your ass off to attain those things. It's not meant to be easy. It's meant to be worth it!

What we do is a critical part of who we are and who we want to become. What you procrastinate or don't act upon, defines you too by determining the person you will never become. I don't understand how it's ok for people to not want to live their best self or create the life of their dreams when we have only one life to live. How could you not want to become the best version of yourself or even worse, how could you not want to work for the things you want in life? I would hate to get old and be on my death bed wishing I would've had the courage to make my dreams come true. I would hate for anyone to have to go through that agony. Live your best life and start now!!

Morning Ritual #5

Right after waking up and consuming any food, drink a huge glass of water at least 16 oz.
Here are five solid reasons to drink a big glass of water right when you wake up.

1. It fires up your metabolism. Studies show that by drinking a big glass of water right after waking up fires up your metabolism by a whopping 24% for 90 minutes.

2. You're dehydrated when you wake up. You just went 7-8 hours without drinking water. Even if you're not feeling thirsty, your body needs the water.

3. Water helps your body flush out toxins. Your kidneys do an amazing job of cleansing and

ridding your body of toxins as long as your intake fluids are adequate. Getting fluids into your body flush out toxins first thing in the morning.

4. Your brain tissue is 75% water. When you're not properly hydrated, your brain operates in less fuel and you can feel drained or experience fatigue or mood fluctuations.

5. It helps reduce body fat. When you aren't taking in enough water, your body can not do its job efficiently. If the only liquids you consume are coffee, tea, sodas and artificial fruit juices , you will become mildly dehydrated forcing your body to slow down its metabolism to compensate. A slow, water-starved metabolism will not burn fat.

Morning Ritual # 6

Get your body moving first thing in the morning!!
Here are a few things you can do to get your energy up:

1. Get a 30-minute cardio session. You can walk around your neighborhood or go for a jog.

2. Join a gym or join a yoga or pilates studio.

If you don't have a gym close by and don't want to go for a jog, you can do this series of exercises instead:

- 100 jumping jacks in your living room
- 100 push ups
- 100 sit-ups

Anything that you do to get the blood pumping I promise will make you feel nourished and extremely energetic. You will love it! Make it a habit to nourish your body every single day!!

"DARKNESS CANNOT DRIVE OUT DARKNESS;
ONLY LIGHT CAN DO THAT. HATE CANNOT
DRIVE OUT HATE; ONLY LOVE CAN DO THAT."

-MARTIN LUTHER KING JR

I CHOOSe TO LIVE BY
CHOICE NOT BY CHANCE

TO BE MOTIVATED
NOT MANIPULATED

TO BE USEFUL
NOT USED

TO MAKE CHANGES
NOT EXCUSES

TO EXCEL
NOT COMPETE

SELF ESTEEM
NOT SELF PITY

TO LISTEN TO MY
INNER VOICE

NOT THE RANDOM
OPINIONS OF OTHERS

Every night before you go to bed I want you to write in your journal. You will set your GOALS & TO-DO list for the following day.

Be specific about your entire day.
For Example:

5:00 am: Wake up time

morning gratitude

morning meditation

make the bed

6:00 am - 7:00 am: Gym.

7:15 am - 8:00 am: Prepare for my work day.

8:30 am - 11:00 am: Work on the task at hand for 2 1/2 hours. Could be a project or writing a book or creating a new program.

11:00 am - 11:25 am: Mandatory nap

12:00 - 1:00 pm: Lunch (I normally use my lunches for meetings)

1:30 pm - 5:30 pm: Coaching Clients, reply to emails, return phone calls.

5:45 pm - 6:30: Social Media Posts and engagement

My evenings are pretty open! I use them to go to the gym again, or go to the movies, bowling, a dancing class, a cooking class, invite people over to my home for a mastermind session. Get creative, do things and hangout with people that ADD MASSIVE AMOUNT OF VALUE to your life.

You can also pick up a great book for the month! Progress brings happiness! Do things that will help you progress in life!!

Mark Your TO-DO list as done every time a task is completed and praise yourself for it.

This exercise is effective. You will feel more accomplished about getting things done. You will also sleep better at night knowing exactly what needs to be done the following day for you to have a successful day.

Do this every single night!!

Stay committed to your growth.

Here is a practice section for you!

Success Daily Planner

5:00 - 6:00 am:

_____

7:00 - 8:00 am:

_____

8:00 - 9:00 am:

_____

9:00 - 10:00 am:

_____

10:00 - 11:00 am:

11:00 - 12:00 pm:

12:00 - 1:00 pm:

1:00 - 2:00 pm:

2:00 - 3:00 pm:

3:00 - 4:00 pm:

4:00 - 5:00 pm:

6:00 - 7:00 pm:

7:00 - 8:00 pm:

8:00 - 9:00 pm:

_____

9:00 - 10:00 pm:

_____

The more specific you are, the better! Write down what you want to accomplish the following day! Check it off once it's completed.

Chapter 4

Your Circle Of Trust

DON'T BE AFRAID OF BEING OUTNUMBERED.
EAGLES FLY ALONE. PIGEONS FLOCK TOGETHER.

DO NOT BE MISLED, BAD COMPANY CORRUPTS
GOOD MORALS.

1 COR. 15:33

This chapter is one of my favorite chapters and I believe one of the most important ones.

Words of WARNING:

To DETOX your life and to keep it clean, you must be selective about who you're hanging out with and who you're getting advice from. In this chapter, I want you to write down the top three people you spend most of your time with and the top three people you are getting your advice from.

Hangout Buddies	Advice Buddies
1.	1.
2.	2.
3.	3.

Now that you have listed your hangout buddies and your advice buddies, I want to ask you a few questions and I want you to be 100% honest about your answers.

Your hangout buddies:

1. How do you spend most of your time with them? (Be specific about the activities you do with them.)

_____

_____

_____

2. Are they helping you to progress in your life? If YES... HOW? If NO... WHY NOT?

_____

_____

_____

3. Do they inspire you to become a better individual? If YES... HOW? If NO... WHY NOT?

_____

_____

_____

4. Do they have big dreams and goals? (Do you know what they are?)

_____

_____

_____

5. Do you aspire to be like them? If yes… WHY?

_____

_____

_____

6. What types of conversations are you having with them? (Be specific.)

_____

_____

_____

_____

_____

_____

_____

_____

I have homework for you. I want you to call these three friends and let them know about this book and what you are doing. Let them know you're doing a DETOXIFY YOUR LIFE PROGRAM. Tell them what this program entails and why you are wanting to do this. See their reaction. Just try it right now. Stop the reading, call them, and I want you to write down what each of them say.

Hangout Buddy 1:

_____

_____

_____

_____

Hangout Buddy 2:

_____

_____

_____

_____

Hangout Buddy 3:

_____

_____

_____

_____

Don't be disappointed or surprised if they don't have a positive reaction, or if they try to tell you you need not to do anything to amplify your life. This is just to give you perspective on their mentality and how they are showing up for you. Or, they might be happy and excited for you. If that's the case, ask them for their full support and accountability. Real friends that love you and want the best for you will always be there to support you when you are wanting to do well in your life.

Now ADVICE BUDDIES:

1. What kind of advice are you requesting from them?

   _____

   _____

   _____

2. Do they have the kind of lifestyle you would like? (houses, cars, toys, vacations)? (If yes please explain, if no, please explain.)

   _____

   _____

   _____

3. Do they have the relationships you would like? (If yes... please explain, if no... please explain.)

   _____

   _____

   _____

4. Do they inspire you? (If yes please explain, if no please explain.

   _____

   _____

   _____

Sometimes we are in so much pain and so desperate for attention and advice that we end up getting advice from the wrong people and it makes our lives worse because when their advice doesn't work, we then find someone to blame. A principle I live by is "Do not take advice from people unless you are willing to trade your life with them."

And if you don't have someone in your life that you look up to, then it's time to start finding new friends and people to hang-out with.

You might be asking yourself, but where do I meet and find new people?

What worked for me was I started going to self-development platforms, workshops, and programs in my area. There are tons across the Country. You must do your research if you're truly committed to your growth. Look on GOOGLE or even FACEBOOK. In the search button, there are multiple "keywords"

you could use to help you in your search.

For EXAMPLE:

- MeetUp.com: good place to find groups in any kind of business.
- Personal Development Courses in my area
- Online Personal Development Courses
- Self-Improvement
- Masterminds in my area
- Business Professionals
- Amplify My Life
- Personal Growth

You can also watch motivational videos in the morning when you're getting ready for the day. This always amps me up and sets my mind up for success!

To find different types of motivational videos, you can go to YouTube and search for:

- Tony Robbins, Lewis Howes, Alexi Panos, Mel Robbins, Jim Rohn, Bob Proctor, Brendon Burchard, Marie Forleo, Esther Perel, Gary Vee, Dean Graziosi, Frank Kern, Ryan Dice, Rich Schefern, Deepok Chopra, Joe Polish, Eben Pagan, Dr. Joe Dispenza,…and I could go on and on.

We have everything available to us at our fingertips. It's up to you to be resourceful, do your research, and take control of the things you want to accomplish in your life.

Part of the problem is that most of us get life advice from people struggling with life themselves. Most of the advice about life we get is from people close to us who either are not happy or are confused and lost with their own life.

You must look beyond the bad advice, look beyond all the noise and confusion. You will soon discover a select group of people who have been in search of an extraordinary life or people who are already creating it.

I have met these people. And it all started when I changed the group of individuals I was hanging out with and getting my advice from.

Be selective who you give your time and energy to. We become a product of our environment, make sure to protect it.

I now surround myself with people who are accomplishing amazing things, people who are creating growth in their own lives, people who are in a constant pursuit of learning and being in service to others.

Chapter 5

Detoxify Your Space

WHEN WE CLEAR THE PHYSICAL CLUTTER
FROM OUR LIVES, WE LITERALLY MAKE WAY
FOR INSPIRATION AND 'GOOD, ORDERLY
DIRECTION' TO ENTER.

- JULIA CAMERON

VIBRATE GOOD ENERGY INTO OTHERS SOULS;
MAKING THEM NEVER FORGET THE BEAUTY OF
YOURS

In this chapter we are going to give your living space a good detox!

I want you to clean up your home. In the space below, write down what rooms you will tackle first in order. Make sure to stick to that order!

For example: kitchen first, master bedroom second, baby room third etc…

1.

2.

3.

4.

5.

6.

In each room, make sure to get rid of things you don't need. The way I do it and what works for me is if I haven't used it in a year, then its trash. This can relate to anything. Clothes, shoes, books, gifts. We hold on to things from the past, and in most cases these things we are holding onto will not allow us to progress. It could be old pictures we are holding onto that do not serve us. Anything that reminds us of pain, or a time in our life that was not good, difficulty... anything with zero value, discard it and never look back. Looking back into your past is like poison. It doesn't serve you!

In each space take a look at your belongings and ask yourself these questions...

1. Do I need this?

2. What's the purpose of keeping this item?

3. Does it serve any value in my life?

4. When was the last time I used it?

5. If I keep it, will I use it anytime soon?

Your space represents your mind. If your place is chaos, then your mind is as well.

You can make this a very fun task! Play some music, listen to a motivational speech, have a reward for yourself once you are done, have a glass of wine or two, dress up in a costume and just have fun while cleaning out your space!! This is meant to be fun! Cheers to new beginnings and a new and improved home!!

Tips on how to clean like a PRO.

The first tip to to clean from the top to the bottom and from left to right. You will do this simultaneously. Left to right or right to left… pick a pattern and stick to it, that way you know you will never miss a spot.

Take all of your cleaning products to the center spot of your space so you are not running back and forth getting products to clean with. Have everything in one bucket in the centered space of the room. This will save you a lot of time!

Also, when using cleaning products… do not spray and wipe immediately, let the products sit for the amount suggested in the back of the bottle. Let the products do their job by spraying and giving them the time to disinfect. Anywhere from 5-10 minutes.

When cleaning your counters in kitchen and bathroom, make sure to go eye level with your counter tops so you don't miss any crumbs that might be on the surface that you haven't seen.

When cleaning your kitchen counter, make sure to also move anything that is sitting on the kitchen counter top. If your microwave is on the counter, make sure to move it and clean underneath and behind it, same thing with the blender or any power pots or containers you make have sitting on the surface of the counter.

There is a nice trick that I like to use when cleaning in general. It's called the S pattern. Instead of cleaning and wiping using the circulation motion, start using the S pattern. From right to left and then the S motion. With the method you are not combining the dirty area with the clean area like you would in the circular motion. Works much more efficiently and you will get amazing results.

When cleaning your home it may look nice and clean but it still looks unorganized. To keep that from happening... any counter tops, bathroom surface or cabinets... you can use the "Paralel/Perpendicular Method". Home stagers across the country use this method for their properties to look nice and tidy! Find your items, pile them up, de-clutter them and line everything up to the ledge of the surface. You can line them up parallel or perpendicular angle, this way it looks much more appealing to the eye.

KITCHEN:
Start with your fridge!
What you will need:

A). All purpose cleaner

B). Micro-fiber cloths

C). Recycling bin

D). Trash can

Step 1: Empty Out Your Fridge

Start by taking everything out of your fridge. Start from top to bottom. Take a look at all of the products, containers and boxes and check for the expiration date. Get rid of anything expired or about to be expired. Also with the products that are about to be expired you can even do some meal prepping that day so they don't go to waste.

Step 1:

First thing you want to do in the kitchen is declutter. Make sure you tidy up and get everything organized and aligned. You first want to start with the dishes. Unload the dishes and make sure your sink is completely clean. Without an unloaded dishwasher and empty sink, you can't properly clean your kitchen. Once you have taken care of the dishes then you want to start decluttering. Move anything that doesn't belong.

At this point grab a small pot of water and place on stove to boil. You will need this boiling water in step 2 of the kitchen cleaning method. Start at 12 o'clock facing the entrance and go clockwise. At this point you can start loading up the dishwasher, start by spray treating the dishes that might be a little bit crusty and place them in the dishwasher. The benefit of working clock wise, is that you get to declutter and tidy as you go and you will have every corner looking organized. This method will prepare you to stage number two. Work your way around bringing everything to the sink and not missing a single corner of your kitchen.

Step 2:

Prep your sink by spraying it with a good disinfectant. Let it sit for 5-10 minutes, then you want to grab the boiling water that you have on the stove top and pour it in the sink and let that sit with the disinfectant for about twenty minutes and then you can flush it with some more hot water at the end of that. Now go back to your twelve o'clock spot by your door and you're going to work your way around the kitchen once again with some cleaning wipes cleaning every area of the surface from top to bottom left to right or right to left. Again; pick a pattern and stick to it so you get better results. As you go make sure you are moving things out of your way and clean behind and underneath them. Don't forget to use the eye level method so you don't miss a spot on the surface before you move on with the cleaning. Once the surface is completely clean you can finish it off with a sealing wet wipe. After you have sealed your counters you can then bring all of the items back to their place.

You can then take a micro fiber cloth and clean your chairs and the kitchen table. Anything that is in your way you can place it in middle of the floor and we will deal with that in section three of your kitchen cleaning.

Section 3: Sink/Floor/Garbage

Make sure you finish up your sink at the very end just in case you have to wash some items through-out your cleaning process.

You can now throw out the garbage, replace the bag and start cleaning the floors. Im old school so I like sweeping and mopping my floors the old fashioned way. You can use whatever method you like best. As you do this make sure you mop your way out of a room, not into a corner.

BATHROOM:

Lets start by decluttering your bathroom!

1. Hair Products that you bought ages ago and haven't used because it didn't work for your hair! This will create a lot more room in your bathroom space.

2. Medicine Cabinet: Go through your medicine cabinet, toss anything that is expired.

3. For the ladies, go through your make up and nail polish... have an honest look at all the products. Get rid of the old products that you have not used in a while. Be honest with yourself. If you haven't used it in 3 months... TOSS IT or give it away to your friends or family.

4. Get rid of bathroom gift sets that you know you're not going to use. DECLUTTER EVERYTHING!

5. Get rid of your old tooth brush. If its 3 months.... Get rid of it and buy yourself a new one.

6. Get rid of your old luffas, sponges or razor blades that look old and dingy.

7. Free samples and travel size items... if you haven't used it in 6 months get rid of it. Stop allowing to take up unnecessary space in your bathroom.

8. Towels and wash cloths: the ones that have holes or stink... toss them out. Only keep towels that look appealing to the eye and that smell nice and clean.

BATHROOM CLEANING:

Items needed:

1. 5 micro-fiber cloths
2. Paper towels to clean the toilet
3. Squeegy for the shower
4. All purpose cleaner and disinfectant
5. Glass Cleaner
6. Tub and tile/ toilet cleaner
7. Baking soda and vinegar if you like going "green"
8. Double sided sponge/ non scratching type
9. Toilet bowl brush
10. Garbage bag
11. Broom Stick
12. Old tooth brush

Part 1:

Tidy/organize the bathroom and pre-treat toilet and shower. Place dirty laundry and towels in the laundry pile. Put scattered items away, throw the garbage out and organize as you go along.

Part 2:

Tackle your vents by creating a high dust using a mop pole and a micro-fiber cloth. Strta dusting from high to low. Tackle all of the areas including the windows. Next tackle your mirrors using a little bit of water on your microfiber and clean them using the S cleaning formula explained earlier in this chapter. Next move on to the counter. Starting from half of the left first and them move on to the right side of the counter. Following the counter make sure to wipe the cover doors and handles.

Next place to tackle will be your medicine cabinet. Make sure you lay a paper towel down on your clean counter, take all of the products inside the cabinet and place them on the paper towel. Shelf by shelf wipe everything and then wipe the products to place them back in the cabinet. Now onto the toilet. Use paper towels to wipe down your toilet. Start from top to bottom wiping every cornet possible. Following the toilet you respray the tub and start scrubbing inside the tub using the S pattern formula. For tile and grub that need some cleaning, you can use some baking soda and toothbrush to scrub the grout line. Then you can rinse the tile walls. If you have a glass shower.. make sure to spray it well and use a brush and microfiber to scrub off excess dirt and then use the squeegy for the final touch.

DECLUTTER YOUR BEDROOM AND CLOSET:

1. EXTRA PILLOWS

2. SOCKS (HOLES OR SINGLE SOCKS TOSS THEM)

3. JEWELRY THAT YOU NO LONGER WEAR OR DISCOLORED OR TANGLED

4. SHOES (GET RID OF THE ONES YOU HAVEN'T USED IN 6 MONTHS

5. NIGHTSTAND JUNK DRAWER (CLEAN IT OUT)

6. BOOKS AND MAGAZINES THAT YOU HAVEN'T READ IN AGES (SEND TO SHELTER OR GIVE AWAY TO FAMILY/ FRIENDS

7. TIES/PURSES (HAVEN'T USED IN 1 YEAR.. TOSS IT)

8. PIT STAINED CLOTHES OR STAINED CLOTHES (DONATE OR TOSS THEM)

9. PLACE ALL OF YOUR CLOTHES ON YOUR BED... IF YOU HAVEN'T WORN IT IN A YEAR.. GET RID OF IT BY DONATING TO A SHELTER OR GIVING AWAY TO THE HOMELESS

10. GET RID OF MISS MATCHED HANGERS

CLEAN YOUR BEDROOM:

HAVE A PLAN AND MAKE SURE TO BE THE RIGHT STATE OF MIND FOR CLEANING. I ALWAYS PUT ON SOME MUSIC OR PLAY MY FAVORITE PODCAST!

CLEANING PRODUCTS NEEDED:
MICROFIBER CLOTHS (3)
GLASS CLEANING CLOTH FOR MIRRORS AND WINDOWS
VACUUM
MOP
ALL PURPOSE CLEANER
GLASS CLEANER
DISINFECTANT
GARBAGE BAG
RECYCABLE BAG
DUSTER
FRESH LINEN

THREE STEPS TO CLEANING YOUR ROOM:

1. THROWING THINGS AWAY OR PUTTING THEM AWAY/ QUICK ORGANIZATION
2. CLEANING, DUSTING DISINFECTING
3. VACUUMING/ SWEEPING/ MOPPING TAKING OUT THE GARBAGE

STEP 1: START BY THE DOOR AND WORK YOUR WAY CLOCKWISE TIDING/ ORGANIZING OR THROWING THINGS AWAY. FOLD ANY CLOTHES THAT ARE AROUND AND PUT THEM AWAY BEFORE GOING INTO THE NEXT STEP.

STEP 2: USE A DUSTER AND DUST EVERY ARE AND CORNER OF YOUR ROOM INCLUDING THE VENTS. THEN START WIPING EVERYTHING FROM TOP TO BOTTOM USING A MICROFIBER

CLOTH. MIRRORS, LAMPS, FRAMES, TABLE TOPS, TV's.

STEP 3: TAKE EVERYTHING OUT OF THE ROOM THE DOES NOT BELONG IN THE ROOM. YOU CAN DEAL WITH THOSE ITEMS ONCE YOU ARE COMPLETELY DONE WITH THE BEDROOM. FINALIZE BY VACUUMING THE ROOM, OR SWEEPING AND MOPPING IF YOU DON'T HAVE RUGS.

ONCE YOU HAVE FINISHED DETOXING YUR HOME MAKE SURE TO REWARD YOURSELF. YOU WILL FEEL 100 POUNDS LIGHTER WALKING INTO A PERFECTLY CLEANED AND ORGANIZED HOME! THIS WILL MAKE YOU FEEL HAPPY & AT PEACE!

Chapter 6

Detoxify Your Thoughts

EVERYONE IS A HOUSE WITH FOUR ROOMS:
PHYSICAL, MENTAL, EMOTIONAL, SPIRITUAL.
UNLESS WE GO INTO EVERY ROOM EVERYDAY,
EVEN IF ONLY TO KEEP IT AIRED, WE ARE NOT A
COMPLETE PERSON.

-RUMMER GODDEN

WATCH YOUR THOUGHTS FOR THEY BECOME
WORDS. WATCH YOUR WORDS FOR THEY
BECOME ACTIONS. WATCH YOUR ACTIONS FOR
THEY BECOME HABITS. WATCH YOUR HABITS,
FOR THEY BECOME YOUR CHARACTER.

-GANDHI

"Watch your thoughts for they become words. Watch your words for they become your actions. Watch your actions for they become habits. Watch your habits, for they become your character." -Gandhi

I repeat this twice on one page because this statement has had a profound impact on my life. This is so true!!!

My questions to you...

What language are you feeding your mind?

What are you telling yourself the moment you wake up?

Is it words of defeat?

Is it words of disappointment?

Is it blame or guilt?

Here is an exercise for you to learn of the nourishment you are feeding your mind.

Mind Nourishment Exercise:

Write down three things that you tell yourself in the morning...

1. _____

2. _____

3. _____

Are these three things serving you in a positive way. If "YES" please explain, if "NO" please explain:

_____

_____

_____

Write down three negative words you consistently use.

1. _____

2. _____

3. _____

Do you feel you are a victim in your life? If "YES" please explain, if "NO" please explain:

_____

_____

_____

_____

_____

_____

If you answered yes, do you believe you can change your paradigm and trust in yourself to become a victor of your circumstances and not a victim? If "YES" please explain, if "NO" please explain:

_____

_____

_____

Here is an assignment to help you get rid of your negative self-sabotaging talk.

It's called "Detoxify Wristbands"

Find a couple of wrist bands. They can be any color, get creative!! This will be a fun exercise, so get ready for the ride and maybe some pain. ;))

You will place a few wristbands on your wrist. This exercise is going to help you become aware of how much negativity comes out of your mouth. Any time you say something negative, it's your duty to slap yourself with the wristband as hard as you can.

You will be very surprised; most people don't know how negative they are until they try this exercise. Create the habit of only speaking positive things. I promise you it will change your life!!!

Avoid:

- Negative Self-talk
- Negative People
- Gossiping
- Negative Remarks
- Negative Environments
- Negative Situations
- Bringing up the past
- Avoid the news
- Avoid negative posts on social media

AVOID ANYTHING NEGATIVE!!!

Now, on a positive note, I want you to write down three positive affirmations you will start telling yourself in the morning. So instead of the negative mumbling in your head, make it a habit to exchange the negative with positive affirmations.

I will give you an example: "I am beautiful and I am powerful and I will accomplish the dreams and goals I have for my life."

Write down three positive affirmations:

1.

_____

_____

_____

2.

_____

_____

_____

3.

_____

_____

_____

Write down three positive people in your life.

1. _____

2. _____

3. _____

What do you like about the people you wrote down? Explain their traits, what do you like about them, and how do they inspire you?

_____

_____

_____

_____

_____

_____

_____

_____

_____

_____

_____

_____

Make it a point to spend time with people that bring out the best in you. We become a product of our environment and the people we hang out with. Protect your space with positivity. Feed your mind positive things always. Even in your bad days, try to look at the beauty in your adversities. Nourish your mind every day!

Here are just a few books that I highly recommend to start on your journey to living a positive and happy life.

- The Four Agreements by Don Miguel Ruiz
- Start With Why by Simon Sinek
- The 7 Habits Of Highly Effective People by Steven R. Covey
- The Power Of Your Subconscious Mind by Joseph Murphy
- The School Of Greatness by Lewis Howes
- High Performance Habits by Brendon Burchard
- Think and Grow Rich by Napoleon Hill
- The Motivation Manifesto by Brendon Burchard

There are so many more, but here are just a few to get you started!

I don't always have time to read, so I downloaded the audible app and I'm constantly feeding my mind with information that is going to amplify my life. When I'm driving I'm listening to a book, when I'm at the gym, I'm listening to a book, when I'm home cleaning, I'm listening to a book. This will change your life if you make it a habit to nurture your mind every single moment you have a chance to.

BECOME OBSESSED WITH YOUR EVOLUTION AND WITH POSITIVITY !!

YOU WILL RECOGNIZE YOUR OWN PATH
WHEN YOU COME UPON IT, BECAUSE YOU
WILL SUDDENLY HAVE ALL THE ENERGY AND
IMAGINATION YOU WILL EVER NEED.

JERRY GILLIES

I LIKE THE DREAMS OF THE FUTURE BETTER
THAN THE HISTORY OF THE PAST.

- THOMAS JEFFERSON

Detox Rock Exercise:

I want you to go outside and search for a beautiful rock. It can be a small rock or a big rock. Make sure it's a rock that inspires you.! This rock will be a symbol in your life. It will represent you, who you are, who you want to become, it will represent your dreams, your goals, and the vision you have for your life.

I want you to grab your journal and write down everything this rock symbolizes in your life.

For EXAMPLE:

My Rock symbolizes POWER, STRENGTH, SUCCESS, LOVE, HOPE, FORGIVENESS, UNDERSTANDING, PEACE.

It also symbolizes the things I want to accomplish in life. Becoming a New York Times #1 Best Seller, winning 1st Place as an IFBB athlete, having my workshops, books, and personal development programs in over 20 Countries in the next 5 years! Help over five million people through my books, workshops, events and online programs. And every day working on becoming a better version of myself.

Write everything you want to accomplish. Be specific, do not be afraid to write your wildest dreams, even if you think people will think you're crazy. That means you're onto something of greatness!

Have it by your bed next to your journal. This rock is your best friend! Wherever you are this rock will be with you. When you're having a bad day or you have negative thoughts I want you to hold your DETOX ROCK in your hand and say out loud what this rock symbolizes.

The PURPOSE of this EPIC exercise is to DETOX your mind of negativity. Get into the habit of creating positive thoughts.

Positive thoughts + Positive Environment = Positive Life. Nobody likes to be around negativity.

Every night and every morning you will hold the Detox Rock in your hand and read from your list what this Detox Rock Means to you.

Commit to yourself and practice this exercise every day. Every time you have a negative thought, pull out your Detox Rock. Proceed to hold your rock in one hand and say the things this Detox Rock represents in your life, and the things you want to accomplish.

Chapter 7

Burying Your Past

History Repeats Itself For those Who Let It

-Stephen r. Covey

Burying the past was one of the most difficult things I have ever done. Not because I didn't want to, but because I didn't know how to. One doesn't realize how poisonous holding on to bad experiences can be. They can irreversibly damage a life if we let them. They can forever stain a soul if we allow it. But the harshest and most detrimental damage they can inflict reside in the devolution of what we are meant to become.

Repeating what we could have done differently over and over again in our heads does nothing to aid in advancement. It's like drinking a glass of poison and expecting the other person to die. Holding on to the past will cost you amazing relationships, experiences, adventures , and it will cost you your life. By letting go of the hurt and madness you will give your life permission to be free and happy!

It happened to me, I forgave the people who wronged me and I forgave myself. I let go of the pain from the past and I never looked back!

I was determined to set my life free of anger, betrayal, dishonesty, abuse, and I was determined to create an extraordinary life!

And so I did!

Burying Your Past Questionnaire:

Step 1: Identify your reasons for burying your past.

1. What are the reasons you want to bury your past?

_____

_____

_____

2. How is your past affecting your life now?

_____

_____

_____

_____

_____

3. How is your past affecting your working conditions?

_____

_____

_____

_____

_____

4. How is your past affecting your relationships/ friendships?

_____

_____

_____

_____

_____

5. How is your past affecting your sex life?

_____

_____

_____

_____

6. How is your past affecting your social life?

_____

_____

_____

_____

7. How is your past affecting your spirit?

_____

_____

_____

_____

8. How is your past affecting the way you view the world?

_____

_____

_____

_____

_____

9. How will your life change once you bury your past?

_____

_____

_____

_____

_____

10. How will it change the status of your relationships?

_____

_____

_____

_____

_____

11. How will it make you feel now that you have decided to commit to this extraordinary decision?

_____

_____

_____

_____

_____

Reading and answering these questions will be your driving force to keep you emotionally committed to this process. You will have struggles and painful emotions will come up, but if your WHY and PURPOSE is strong enough, you will stay committed!

Second Step is to identify your emotions. Our emotions drive our life. We are not aware of our negative reactions that stem from the past. Your emotional habits can destroy you or make you. They affect the way you speak, act and the way you carry yourself.

Learn how to empower the positive and disempower the negative.

Becoming aware of your emotional habits, you can create the shift needed to create extraordinary experiences in your life. Your emotions are like a muscle: you can train yourself to feel depressed, stressed, sad or even frustrated or you can do the complete opposite and train yourself to feel passion, joy, love and laughter. The more you condition your mind, the more attached to you those emotions become.

Step 2: Identify Your Negative Emotional Habits: (Emotional Assessment)

In this exercise you will circle the negative habits that apply to you. And then you will rate the bad habit from a scale of 1-10... 1 being the least negative. (Be honest with yourself.)

1. I am my own worst critic.

    1   2   3   4   5   6   7   8   9   10

2. I push people away.

    1   2   3   4   5   6   7   8   9   10

3. I don't eat healthy and I don't exercise.

    1   2   3   4   5   6   7   8   9   10

4. I don't get enough sleep.

    1   2   3   4   5   6   7   8   9   10

5. I speak negative to myself and about myself.

    1   2   3   4   5   6   7   8   9   10

6. I sabotage myself.

    1   2   3   4   5   6   7   8   9   10

7. I don't apologize when I should.

    1   2   3   4   5   6   7   8   9   10

8. I give into moodiness instead of practicing reliability.

    1   2   3   4   5   6   7   8   9   10

9. I worry about what I stand to gain instead of taking responsibility.

    1   2   3   4   5   6   7   8   9   10

10. I wait for something to happen instead of creating a momentum.

    1   2   3   4   5   6   7   8   9   10

11. I allow my attitude to take control of me instead of the other way around.

    1   2   3   4   5   6   7   8   9   10

12. I chase what feels good instead of doing what's right.

    1   2   3   4   5   6   7   8   9   10

13. I do what's convenient instead of doing what's right.

    1   2   3   4   5   6   7   8   9   10

14. I place judgement on others.

    1   2   3   4   5   6   7   8   9   10

15. I'm not staying committed to the things I say I'm going to do.

    1   2   3   4   5   6   7   8   9   10

16. I think I'm a failure.

    1   2   3   4   5   6   7   8   9   10

17. I live with regret.

    1   2   3   4   5   6   7   8   9   10

18. I'm a people pleaser.

    1   2   3   4   5   6   7   8   9   10

19. I seek attention to feel good about myself.

    1   2   3   4   5   6   7   8   9   10

20. I like gossiping about other people.

    1   2   3   4   5   6   7   8   9   10

Now that you have completed this exercise we are going to do an evaluation to see where you stand on your negative emotional assessment.

Before you continue, add all the numbers you circled. Write your total number in this space_____.

Score Board:

160+: You have some work to do. Focus on changing your negative paradigms. By the time you have reached this section in this manual, you should know the new habits you need to start implementing to make drastic positive changes in your life!

120 to 160: You have improvements to make but you're not bad. Take baby steps in improving the quality of your life, it all doesn't have to happen in one day. Progress brings happiness, stay committed and focused to your goals. You have nothing to lose and everything to gain.

120 or less: You are doing great! However, in order to continue feeling and doing great, you must continue to explore and be on a constant pursuit of growth and evolution. Never get comfortable. If you snooze you will lose!

If you have a high score, don't beat yourself up! Now you are aware and you know the changes you need to make in order to change your negative habits. Progress brings happiness, so start implementing the changes little by little. and get ready to watch your life transform in ways you never thought possible.

Step 3: Forgiveness Definition

Forgiveness is the intentional and voluntary process by which a victim undergoes a change in feelings and attitude regarding an offense, lets go of negative emotions such as vengefulness, with an increased ability to wish the offender well.

Forgiveness is powerful!

Forgiveness allows you to free your soul of any darkness. Forgiveness turns pain into healing and peace. It can help you overcome negative feelings and relational conflicts. I know for some people this is hard to do. But once you make the conscious decision of letting go of that anger and grudge, you will feel a huge weight lifted off of your shoulders. People are not aware of how detrimental to your life un-forgiveness can be. It's like feeding a plant gasoline and expecting it to flourish. That is what you're doing to your soul, your poisoning it.

You might be thinking " why would I want to forgive anyone who has harmed me?"

It's not about forgiving a person and then allowing them back in to your life and letting them harm you again. It's about setting yourself free so you can move forward in your life. It means giving up the suffering of the past and willing to move forward with greater potential and inner freedom. Forgiveness means letting go of the past.

Forgiveness requires an in depth thought and conversation within ourselves.

If you feel stuck and you don't know how or where to start your forgiveness journey, here are a few exercises that helped me in my forgiveness process.

A). Identify the people who have wronged you and you have not forgiven. Write a list of them.

_____

_____

_____

_____

_____

_____

_____

_____

B). Write down what each of them did that caused
   you pain. (Be Specific)

_____

_____

_____

_____

_____

_____

_____

_____

_____

_____

_____

_____

_____

_____

_____

_____

How have these betrayals or hurts made you feel. Be detailed and specific about each of them. LET IT ALL OUT!

_____

_____

_____

_____

_____

_____

_____

_____

_____

_____

_____

_____

_____

_____

_____

_____

_____

_____

_____

_____

_____

_____

C). Write down how each betrayal has affected
   your life. (Be specific)

_____

_____

_____

_____

_____

_____

D). Is this anger and resentment worth your happiness and peace of mind?

_____

_____

_____

_____

_____

E). Have you found any lessons from these painful memories? If yes, please explain.

_____

_____

_____

_____

_____

_____

F). Do you think forgiving will set you free and bring you peace? If yes, please explain how.

_____

_____

_____

_____

_____

_____

G). Are you willing to forgive 100% whole heartedly? Please explain.

_____

_____

_____

_____

_____

_____

These questions are asked to give you perspective. To allow you identify your trigger points so you are aware on how not forgiving is detrimental to your growth.

Forgiveness Mission Statement:

If you are committed to Forgiveness,

write your name in the blank space below. Date and sign at the bottom.

I _____ have decided to forgive those who have wronged me. I no longer carry this pain and weight on my shoulders. I choose to forgive for my own peace of mind, so that I can continue creating a life of freedom, happiness, and abundance. There is no place for hatred, revenge, or darkness in my life. I will no longer be a victim of unforgiveness.

I will stay true to myself and to my commitment. This is my truth and I will honor it!

_____

SIGN

_____

DATE

Congratulations on making the decision to forgive! IT'S ONE OF THE BEST DECISIONS I EVER MADE!!!

STEP 4: Train your mind to work for you and not against you.

Now that you have stopped the self-sabotaging. I am going to show you how to have the ultimate breakthrough by conditioning your mind every single day. It's a daily commitment and practice. There is no such thing as perfection, therefore you will have your days where you feel defeated, or not in the mood, or you're feeling doubtful and questioning yourself. This is normal, however, do not allow your mind to stay in this state. You can condition your mind to get out of these negative emotions. You decide what goes into your mind. You must stand guard at the door of your mind and protect it. Feed yourself empowering thoughts, surround yourself with amazing people who make you a better person. It's the smallest rituals that you implement every day that will build momentum and ultimately, lead to massive change.

I want you to write a personal mission statement.

A Personal Mission Statement defines who you are, what you are about, and it defines what's valuable to you.

My Personal Mission Statement reads like this:

"I am Melitsa Waage. I'm a transformational thought leader. I empower people to reach their peak potential by shifting their mindsets to overcome any self-limiting beliefs. I value loyalty, integrity, freedom, and love. I believe we all hold the power to create a life of abundance and fulfillment."

When writing your Personal Mission Statement, I want you to define your values and principals.

Answer the following questions to help you form your (PMS):

- Who are you?

- What are you about?

- What do you value?

Personal Mission Statement: (PMS)

_____

_____

_____

_____

_____

_____

_____

_____

Congratulations on writing your PMS! This is who you are, what you represent, and what you value! Anytime you find yourself struggling with your emotions, I want you to say your PMS and remind yourself that you are more powerful than your thoughts and you have the power to get back to a positive state of mind. You are in control of your emotions, not the other way around. Condition your mind to repeat your PMS every single day. Use your PMS as a reminder of the dreams and goals you have for your life. Stay focused and committed to your evolution.

DON'T EVER GIVE UP!

Step 5: Burying Your Past Statement:

If you are committed to Burying your past,
    write your name in the blank space below and date and sign at the bottom.
    I _____ have made the decision to bury my past and never let my past affect my life and take away my happiness. I value who I am and what I stand for. I'm not a victim of my past, I am a victor. I am in control of my thoughts and my emotions. I stand at the gate of my mind and I will allow only empowering thoughts which will aid in the transformation of my life.

_____

SIGN

_____

DATE

Congratulations on making this extraordinary decision of burying your past.

You will now start to look at life with a whole new set of lenses. Appreciating and living in gratitude! Focus on your happiness and your dreams. Spend time with the people that matter most to you, spend time doing things you love, read a book, write a book, create something new in your life.

You are the author and creator of your own life story. Make it one worth reading! It's all up to you. You're on to a great start!!! I believe in you!

Chapter 8

Living in Gratitude

GRATITUDE MAKES SENSE OF OUR PAST, BRINGS
PEACE FOR TODAY, AND CREATES A VISION FOR
TOMORROW.

-MELODY BEATTIE

GRATITUDE IS RICHES. COMPLAINT IS POVERTY.

-DORIS DAY

I believe GRATITUDE should be one of the fundamentals of our lives. When you live in a constant state of gratitude, there is no room for fear, anger, depression, negativity. Practicing gratitude is like watering your plants for them to continue to grow and blossom. Whatever you focus on expands! Worry is an action. Gratitude is an action. Both are optional. By choosing gratitude, you drive out the space and time for worry.

When you neglect the action of appreciating, you limit your potential for joy and contentment in the present moment. Worry does not prevent bad things from happening; it only prevents you from accessing joy at this moment.

There are moments when I get upset and I'm not feeling my best. I'm definitely not perfect and not pretending to be... however, a few of the secrets that I use to make myself feel better when I'm feeling this way are:

1. I look for a homeless person and I buy them a meal.

2. I think of the children dying in their hospital beds.

3. I think of the families that today will get that horrible phone call they lost a loved one.

4. I give someone I love a call and let them know they are in my thoughts.

5. I take out my journal and write down five things I'm grateful for and why I'm grateful for them.

6. I say my affirmations out loud ... "I am beautiful", "I am powerful", "I'm destined for greatness and nothing will stop me".

7. I go work-out.

8. I go to YOUTUBE and find myself a motivational video to get me excited!

These are ways I also practice gratitude! This is a daily habit for me. First thing I do in the morning when I wake up is write down a list of 5 things I'm grateful for and why. It starts my day on a positive high.

For example:

1. Today I'm grateful for another day of life! This new opportunity allows me to continue to serve and be a beacon of hope, love, and transformation in people's lives.

2. I'm grateful for the food I'm about to consume throughout the day. I feel blessed it's available to me whenever and wherever I choose.

3. I'm grateful for the roof over my head. It's my sanctuary I call my home. I'm blessed beyond belief that I have a home.

4. I'm grateful for my businesses, books, masterminds, workshops, and events. I'm living my passion and fulfilling my purpose while I'm here on earth.

5. I'm thankful for the people I encounter throughout my days. My goal is to create a positive impact in their lives, even if it's just for a minute of speaking to them.

My gratitudes change every single day! There is so much to be grateful for! I even write down things that have never happened and I want them to happen. Me writing them down is my heart manifesting what I want into the universe! Whatever you focus on expands. So, I focus and give thanks for the things I want to call into my life. I'm grateful that I live in a country where there is complete freedom and I can express myself however I choose to. I'm lucky and blessed I'm not stuck in a third world country with no food or home. I can keep on going and going, but

I'm sure you get my point. The gratitude habit has changed my life and I know it will change yours once you make this a ritual!! Try it right now!! Write down five things you're grateful for and why.

<u>Gratitude Exercise:</u>

1.

_____

_____

_____

_____

_____

2.

_____

_____

_____

_____

3.

_____

_____

_____

_____

4.

_____

_____

_____

_____

_____

5.

_____

_____

_____

_____

_____

This habit has allowed me to live the life that I have now. A foster child with a troubled past that was never supposed to amount to anything.

Yet, here I am wanting to share my story and help people transform their lives! WE ARE ALL CREATED FOR GREATNESS!

Never forget that!

Chapter 9

Meet Your Future Self

LOVE YOURSELF ENOUGH TO CREATE THE
BEST VERSION OF YOU! EVOLUTION OF THE
MIND, BODY, AND SOUL IS THE KEY TO THE
DISCOVERY OF YOUR LIFE'S MISSION!

-MELITSA WAAGE

In this chapter, I want to take you on a journey. A journey into the unknown you will create with your imagination and visualizing your future. I want you to meet your future self twenty years from now. I want you to visualize your future and who you want to become. You must picture yourself where you'd like to be in twenty years from now. The daily practice of visualizing your dreams as already accomplished will rapidly accelerate your achievement of those dreams, goals and ambitions.

Here are four important benefits of using visualization techniques.

1. It gives you clarity and taps into your creative subconscious, which will generate creative ideas for you to accomplish your goals.

2. You reprogram your brain to think of your dreams every day and recognize what you must do to see these dreams come to fruition.

3. It inspires you and motivates you to do whatever it takes to make your dreams a reality.

4. It powers up the law of attraction, manifesting and drawing into your life people, resources, and circumstances that will be valuable in achieving your goals.

<u>Future Self Exercise:</u>

For this exercise, you must be in a dark place with no distractions. Turn off your ringer, lock your door and make sure to not be disturbed by anything or anyone.

Close your eyes and envision yourself walking to a river, and in the river there is a small boat waiting for you. There is a captain waiting to take you to meet your future self. Enter the boat and take a seat. The boat starts its journey through the dark grey water. It's windy outside with cloudy skies. As your waiting to get to your destination, I want you to think of your life and the things you have done so far.

- Are you happy with yourself?
- Are you happy with the life you have created?
- Are you proud of the person you see in the mirror?
- Have you given your all in life?
- Are you fulfilled with the things you have done?
- What will you tell your future self when you meet each other?

You are almost approaching your destination…

I want you to envision what kind of house your future self owns. This is the house you will enter to meet you twenty years from now.

The boat stops and the captain is letting you out. He tells you he will pick you up in an hour from now.

You're standing in front of your home.

What does it look like? (Be specific)

_____

_____

_____

What color is the front door?

_____

_____

_____

What color is the house?

_____

_____

_____

Is it a two-story home or single-family home?

_____

_____

_____

How big is the yard?

_____

_____

_____

How many car garages does it have?

_____

_____

_____

Is it the house of your dreams?

_____

_____

_____

Now, after observing your home... walk towards your door and knock.

Your door opens and it's your future self who answers.

What do you look like?

_____

_____

_____

Are you healthy and fit?

_____

_____

_____

Are you looking the way you would want to look in twenty years from today?

_____

_____

_____

What colors are the clothes your future self is wearing?

_____

_____

_____

Are you impressed with yourself?

_____

_____

_____

Are you happy with your future self's appearance?

_____

_____

_____

What are the first words your future self tells you?

_____

_____

_____

Walk in to have a chat with your future self.

What does the inside of your home look like?

_____

_____

_____

What are the colors?

_____

What does it smell like?

_____

_____

_____

Do you like what you see?

_____

_____

_____

Is there music playing in the background?

_____

If yes, what kind of music is it? Who is the artist or band?

_____

_____

_____

Take a seat in your living room.

What does your living room look like? (Be specific)

_____

_____

_____

Are there paintings on the wall?

_____

If yes, what kind of paintings are they? What are the colors?

_____

_____

_____

What color is your couch?

_____

_____

_____

What does your couch feel like? Is it leather, suede, silk...?

_____

_____

_____

Take a seat.

What is your conversation like? (Be specific)

_____

_____

_____

What words of wisdom is your future self sharing with you?

_____

_____

_____

_____

What fears and battles is your future self telling you to let go of?

_____

_____

_____

_____

_____

What people in your life right now is your future self telling you that you must left go of for you to progress in life?

_____

_____

_____

_____

_____

What kind of advice is your future self giving you?

_____

_____

_____

_____

_____

What kind of endeavors is your future self telling you you must start?

_____

_____

_____

_____

TIME IS UP!

It's time for you to go back to the boat and begin your journey back home.

But before you leave your future self and your future home...

Your future self wants to give you a gift for you to take back.

Your future self hands you a box. This gift is meant to inspire you and must be used as a token of prosperity and progression in your life.

Open the box. What gift has your future self given you?

_____

_____

Take your gift with you and leave your future home and future self.

How are you feeling this very moment now that you have met yourself twenty years from now?

_____

_____

_____

What feelings and emotions came up for you with this exercise?

_____

_____

_____

_____

_____

Are you proud of the future self you met?

_____

_____

_____

_____

_____

What are you going to do differently in your life now that you have met your future self?

_____

_____

_____

_____

_____

This exercise makes you realize how important it is for you to take action now! This is a must! Life will pass you by and before you know it, twenty years have passed and you have accomplished nothing. You don't want this to be you! Take your life seriously! Take action today! I want to see you succeed, I want to see you create a life of abundance, fulfillment, and happiness.

Don't you want to feel complete? Don't you want to feel proud of yourself? Don't you want to give it your all? Don't you want to set an example to those who follow you?

I know you do!

When I first did this exercise, I cried once I was done. I saw the vision I have for my life reveal itself in front of me. I created it, I worked hard for it. The woman that opened the door and greeted me was strong, accomplished, powerful! Her skin was glowing, love a prosperity surrounded her, she smelled like a garden of happiness and success! She was complete and fulfilled. She inspired me, she became my hero!

If you can visualize it, you can make it a reality!!!

Chapter 10

Creating Your Legacy

"WHAT ARE YOU WILLING TO DO TO CREATE
THE LIFE OF YOUR DREAMS?"

- Melitsa Waage

What is a legacy?

Leaving a legacy is the need or the desire to be remembered for what you have contributed to the world. Sometimes, that contribution can be so special that the universe is unalterably changed the world.

What does it mean to leave a legacy? It means having a mark on the future and contributing for future generations to come.

Getting clear and specific about your legacy will be will help you with the following:

- Once you are certain what you want your legacy to be, you can create it.
- Having clarity on your legacy will give your life purpose and meaning.
- It will inspire you daily in a positive way.
- It will allow you to show up every day as a confident and dedicated individual who is inspired and determined to create a positive impact in this world.
- You will live your life as if you matter.

- You can live the way you want to be remembered.
- You will do and create things that matter now.
- You will let go of the negativity in your life.

Look at your legacy as the most powerful statement you have ever written.

You are the author and creator of your own life story. In a few words explain how you want to be remembered.

See yourself as the President of the United States. What will you create in the next four years? How will you impact our beautiful Nation in a positive way? How will you want your people to talk about you? How will you set up this Country for success for the following President? What will he have to say about the positive impact and change you have created? How do you want your Presidency to be remembered? What will be missed about you? What positive attributes will they associate with you?

Here is an exercise to help you identify and create the legacy you want to leave for generations to come:

A). What will you create for your life in the next year? (Be as detailed as possible)

_____

_____

_____

_____

_____

_____

_____

_____

_____

_____

_____

_____

_____

_____

_____

_____

_____

CARVE YOUR NAME ON HEARTS, NOT
TOMBSTONES. A LEGACY IS ETCHED INTO THE
MINDS OF OTHERS AND THE STORIES THEY
SHARE ABOUT YOU.

- SHANNON L. ALDER

Chapter 11

Closing Chapter

Conquering my mind was one of the hardest things for me to do, struggling with negative thoughts, negative behaviors that were not serving me well, and battling with myself every day was exhausting. It wasn't until I realized that I had to change my daily habits, my "friendships" my environments for me to create a serious deep transformation in my life.

It takes a lot of hard work, determination, and the will to never give up on yourself in order to change your life and have it work for you and not against you. It's difficult! You will have your distractions, you will have your days where you want to give up, you will have fears, doubts and insecurities will arise. But you must stay strong and not forget the vision you have for your life! This is crucial and important.

How are you wanting to show up in this world? How are you wanting to show up for your family and the people that mean the most to you? How do you want to be remembered? You must not lose track of that clarity just because you have a few bumps in the road I know will come up. Have that clarity stamped on your forehead and don't lose track. Remember everything you have learned throughout this book. In your moments of weakness… you will have them… I want you to grab this book and go back to the pages where you wrote your goals, where you wrote down the person you want to become, where you wrote down the vision for your life. Go back to the chapters where you made an oath of forgiveness, where you wrote down your Personal Mission Statement (PMS). If your past still comes back to haunt you, go back to Chapter seven where you promised to let go of the past.

Don't just put this book in a closet where you will never see it again, place it in a place where you see it every time you wake up and every time you go to bed. Have it as a reminder of the promises you have made to yourself. Have it as a reminder of the things you want to call into your life. Stay committed to your growth, stay committed to your evolution. Creating an extraordinary life is not meant to be easy, but once you have mastered your mind it will start to become much easier, you will become much better at everything you do. Progress brings happiness!

You must care enough about your life to learn new things, to live in service with who you want to become, and care enough to learn about others and to be of contribution to this world.

You must love yourself enough to take action right now!!! No more wasting time, no more excuses, no more blaming others for your problems or your failures. Take responsibility for your own life! Walk the talk, show up with courage, show up with conviction, show up with gratitude, show up like the person you want your children to marry one day.

Nobody will come and save you. This might sound harsh, but it is the truth! Stop waiting for permission to start creating the life of your dreams, because nobody will give it to you. It's your personal responsibility to improve and control your own behaviors and your own life. Without massive action, your dreams will stay dreams and just a wanting in your memory and that leads to depression and sadness in the long-run.

You can read all the personal development articles, books, and blogs. But if you don't take massive action, all that effort is a huge waste of time.

You must apply what you have learned in this book! Reading this book will make you feel good and empowered, but it's the actions and steps you must take once you are done reading it. Always remember, progress brings happiness! Once you implement and you achieve, you will become addicted to the feeling of accomplishment and success. You will want more and you will demand more of your life. You will want to inspire others and invite others on your journey, you will want to share your happiness and excitement with the world. The world is waiting for you. The world is waiting for you to step into your super-power.

I wrote this book with so much love and passion in my heart. I want people to know and believe that no matter what has happened in your life you can overcome your obstacles and use them as a source of strength and growth to progress in your life. When we are going through our darkest moments, we don't get it. We hate our lives and we hate everything that is happening around us. But you must take a moment and relax your mind and think of the lessons your adversities are trying to teach you. If you don't learn from your adversities, it will keep happening repeatedly.

In your moments of darkness and frustration, remember that you are not alone. You have people that love you and care for you. In your moments of darkness, pick up the phone and call a friend or a loved one and let them know that you need them. Nothing is wrong with being vulnerable. It's ok. I understand your pain.

I was a foster child from the age of three. My biological parents were heroin addicts, they lost their three kids to this horrible addiction. I spent years in the foster care system. I remember at first going to different homes feeling afraid, alone, humiliated that nobody loved me. For many years I had anger in my heart. I was mad at the world because I wasn't a "normal" child. I wanted my own mom and dad and I didn't want to feel that sense of rejection that I was waking up with every single day. I hated my life and I hated my childhood. I finally found a family that took me in. Even though they had great intentions with me, I hated them. I felt rejected and didn't feel good enough. I tried to hurt myself twice because I thought that was the only way of me getting noticed. I was miserable and I resented them for it.

I left that home at the age of fifteen.

My future didn't look bright. I was surrounding myself with bad influence and making bad decisions. I became homeless and lived out of my car. I then got kicked out of high school and was told by my principal I would never amount to anything. I remember feeling like I wanted to quit my life. I was lost, confused, and afraid. Every person I had loved had betrayed me and I had nowhere to go. My trunk was full of my clothes, pillows, and blankets. I was taking showers at the Disney resorts in Orlando, FL. That's where I lived. At night I would park in a Walmart parking lot underneath a big light post with a camera on it. I did that in case anything happened to me, it would be on film. Wow, that was a dark moment in my life. It was scary and terrifying. But guess what??? I never gave up!!! I brought myself out of that dark whole. I worked towards creating a better life for myself. I sought ways to better my life and I was on a mission to create great things. I moved to NYC to pursue a modeling and music career. Although I was doing well with it, I was not passionate about it. That industry didn't inspire me and I wanted more out of my life.

I then met my ex-husband who I fell madly in-love with and I dropped everything I was doing in NYC to move to Miami Florida and start a Real Estate business while also working as a VIP host at some of the hottest night clubs in South Beach. The money I was making allowed me to Invest in my first company, a Real Estate Firm called "Visual Investments". I became an entrepreneur by the age of 24. I was excited and felt I had the World in my hands. By the looks of it, we would be millionaires in a few years. But then reality hit us in the face and the Real Estate market collapsed and we lost it all. My hopes and dreams were shattered once again.

But then I said to myself, there has to be a better way. This was the time where MY SPACE became a huge hit.

Then suddenly it was as if a light bulb hit my head. I was once again excited!!! I told my former husband, let's start an internet company and call it "The Pro Stylist". We created a beauty platform for the beauty industry to advertise their products and services. Being young entrepreneurs with zero experience in the online world, we created and invested all of my money for about 4 years with the wrong people and developers. We created a solid business plan and pitched it to every angel investor we would find out about. We got online and searched countless times for people to help us. We were relentless in our search. We wouldn't take no for an answer. Blood, sweat, and tears were our daily struggle. We were running out of money and we were afraid and scared. Nothing was working and nobody wanted to invest.

But one day finally, we found an angel investor that saw what we saw. He saw the vision we had for our company. He knew what needed to be done to get our company off the ground and make it generate a profit for us. We changed the name of the company and called it "Hair Society."

We trusted this man with everything we had. In our desperation, we didn't take the proper steps we needed when handling business transactions. This man promised us the world with no contract. We saw progress in the development and launch of our baby, so we trusted him and handed over all of our intellectual property and all of the secret ingredients that made up our company awesome.

Long story short, this man disappeared from our lives with everything. Just like that. Nowhere to be found. No calls, no emails, nowhere to find him. Once again, my world crumbled at my feet. Five years of hard work, over 100k of my own money invested into this projected... all vanished. Once again being betrayed by someone I trusted.

Honestly, we didn't know what to do. We felt embarrassed, afraid, confused and had nowhere to turn to. I thought the tragedy had ended there. But not long after, I lost my marriage due to betrayal. I talk about this in Chapter 2 "There is Beauty in the Storm."

My best friend, my "soul-mate," my world at the time, cheated on me. I was crushed, devastated, embarrassed, alone, and I honestly had nowhere to go. This tore my soul into pieces. I hated everyone and everything. Once again, betrayed by someone I loved. I spent the next year being self-destructive and hanging out with the wrong crowd. It was my way of dealing with the heartache. I was out every night, drinking, and not doing anything positive in my life. I was in a dark hole. A dark hole of depression, sadness, shame, and guilt. I was blaming everything on myself. I was trying to figure what I could have done different so none of this would have happened.

But one day, I woke up and said "enough is enough!" No more self-pity, no more sadness, no more blaming. No more destroying my life! I have too much love to give.

That is where my journey began in the Personal Development world. I sought ways to better my life, I sought better people to surround myself with. I became a student of life, researching programs to help me to tap into my greatness and help me figure out my super power.

I have spent the last four years investing in myself. Going around the Country attending workshops and becoming part of programs that have changed my life. At first I was skeptical about these courses and I first thought they just wanted my money. But when I invested a few dollars on my first course, and I saw the positive impact it had in my life, I became addicted to Personal Development. I implemented the things I was learning in these workshops, I lived by their teachings.

The individuals I was meeting at these events were on the same path as me. They were looking for growth, they were looking for a better life, they were looking for freedom and inner peace. We were on the same mission. These individuals have turned out to be the best friends a person could ever ask for. A lot have turned their lives around and have created multi-million-dollar corporations. They have become published authors, motivational speakers, entrepreneurs, social media influencers. They have inspired me to step into my greatness and share my story with the world. They have become my accountability partners. Nothing bad has ever come out of investing in my growth and joining these platforms. My life has been amplified.

If this is the first personal development book you have ever picked up, please don't stop. Continue searching for more, continue learning, continue mastering your life, learn how to become epic, learn how to create greatness, learn the value of your soul. I promise you and assure you, the more you seek, learn, and apply… the more you will find the answers to your life you have been seeking. You will feel fulfilled, you will learn how to love every inch of you. You will learn how to master your life and create a life worth living.

Take this advice from someone like me. A foster child abandoned and neglected, a homeless living out of my car, a failed entrepreneur many times over, a woman betrayed by her husband, an individual that has been on life support.

If I can go through these things and be here making an impact in this world, then so can you.

Things don't happen to you, they happen for you.

Allow your struggle to serve you. Allow your pain to teach you and push you in the right direction.

I wrote this book to inspire you!

No matter what hardships you have gone through, follow the simples tools in this book and transform your life right now. I know it will work for you because it worked for me. This is how I live my life every day!

Welcome to my journey!

Feel free to reach out to me. Message me if you have questions, message if you need some guidance, message me if you need support. You are not alone. I created this book for you.

Thank you for receiving my gift.

With lots of love in my heart,

Melitsa Waage.

CPSIA information can be obtained
at www.ICGtesting.com
Printed in the USA
LVHW052156180520
655844LV00004B/346